SAPPHO'S *GYMNASIUM*

SAPPHO'S *GYMNASIUM*

OLGA BROUMAS & T BEGLEY
WITH A RAPTURE BY KAZIM ALI

NIGHTBOAT BOOKS
NEW YORK

This edition published by Nightboat Books in 2017
All rights reserved
Printed in the United States of America

ISBN 978-1-937658-59-5

Design and typesetting by Margaret Tedesco
Text set in Optima and Palatino Linotype
Cover art, T Begley: *Untitled*, 2013. Acrylic media, photographic fragments
Courtesy of the artist

Cataloging-in-publication data is available
from the Library of Congress

Distributed by University Press of New England
One Court Street
Lebanon, NH 03766
www.upne.com

Nightboat Books
New York
www.nightboat.org

CONTENTS

PROEM

Sappho's Gymnasium: Tears unbecome the house of poets.
                                    —Sappho to Kleis, on not mourning

Gymn: nude, trained, exposed, athletic, flexible, practice.
Gymnasteon: imperative practice: tears unbecoming.

Ink where to care, founder of joy: ancestral, historical, female, only.

"I threw my whole self into psychagogia. I danced, I sang, I was
in plays. I made up my mind and so did a lot of the youngest girls.
I was 16. You tried to give something, a sweet note, to cheer the rest
of the camp. We paid in beatings and solitary. We never put the
banner down. Released from solitary, start singing, then solitary
again. In and out. Solitary and singing."
        —Plousia L., speaking about her incarceration by the Gestapo at
one of the island prison camps: Icaria, Chios, Trikeri, Makronisos.
Compiled by Janet Hart, in Women in the Greek Resistance.

Psychagogia: soul rearing.

". . . in unequal battle the whole human comes awake. Also the poet.
The idea of a book held me as icons hold others. I saw it and turned
its pages. The poems I had not written and would have wanted to write
filled its pages with their external shape. I had but to 'fill it' as you
fill a row of empty glasses and, immediately, what power, what
freedom, what disdain toward bombs and death it gave me."
        —The second great Lesbian, Odysseas Elytis.

1

Trust so broad we cash chromosomes
praising floor carried into fields a synonym of life
I shall be all with her and protect her
from any harm and shall defend her in the midst of peace

Call inexplicable ex spirit mental

"What prevents you from doing your work has become your work."
                                                    —Albert Camus

Urge, work, energy, orgasm, worship: common root ourg.

Aphrodytian celebrants: therapaenidae.
Roots: ther: summer harvest, heat, nourish, and
Poio: poet, creator, god.
Therapist: homophonic.
Therapaenis. Postdoxic: prostitute.

Narrative comforts — you skim it.
Roland Barthes: "any completed utterance runs the risk of being ideological."

Gymnosophist imperative: antonym clutter.

Grief under anger, doxa interrupts praise; constant grief: just depression.

Narrative: doxa: thought police: recorded grammar.

Aphrodytian Prelapsarian Predoxic grammar: pupil only to you, fleece of dew.

Who speaks? Metis, Outis. But, who speaks?

A voice of pluracination, gracing one of us with particulars, the other with the hallucinated breath of verbally unintelligible but musically incontrovertible dictions.

That was one time, which recurs. Another is certitude of the field it requires us to serve: eros: gracious, philoxenous, augmenting, lubricant faith.

We dwell, like most, in the lugubrious, cacophonous chaos of the imperial globe absorbed in its Babel complex. We don't have to sing about it.

"That which disempowers you is unfit for your song."
                                        —Odysseas Elytis

The lyric refuses its raptor. Sappho's legacy to her daughter Kleis, her gymnasium, is "Tears unbecome the house of poets."

Our translation honors Sappho's lithe tongue, if not the exact plurality of her meaning. Her word for 'tears' is 'thren', the root of lamentation (as in threnody), which is onomatopoeic and doesn't imply words (why ode is needed in threnody).

Thren' is the sonoric and somatic act of lamentations.

For "unbecome" she uses ou Themis, (not Themis), the female god of Justice and ethics. What occurs in the simple swap is pleasure. Pleasure is infant; it too saves nothing.

I mean the nothing that would have us undergo a surgery wherein "all light" is the only possible and desirable transplant.

"Few know the emotional superlative is formed of light, not force,"
—Sappho's island-mate through millennia, Odysseas Elytis.

My skin is the volunteer cipher of your emotion. Who speaks?
Collaboration is compassion. Erasure of "ego" and "muse."

OPTICA

Across the seascape
the fountains running

I could get very close
to the ruins before they would start

and retreat
into my study the herds travel from

whiteness to whiteness
the voiceless farther out scarred with ravines

outplaying doxa
on broken tablets the groves

prevent the eye from stopping

the Helens
helical in their throes

rotate the picture plane
spin the window into the window

you are shadow
hello shadow

beautiful statue whose outflow
I smuggle out for you

Flight of stones above the first
chronographic Minervas

blue in the custody
the mobile dervish your nails mark

throughout without perishing
your discourse

shapeable seeds words
cuttings this stem

founded in limestone
oxygen careening through a volume of stars

computations hallucinatory
to arrange G

forces I carve Dactyls
Greek names of the sea that grape

& honey philosophy
aporias the self

one jouissance of language
with melancholy porcelain jump & crack

of demolition
hammering bird on a line of flight

thrown a whiteness
dimension outside contact

caritas I have been

you and pick you
up the strands

surf to my gate break
across my garden

Expanse of indigo riven by orphic nerves

in the picture's small square
distances of Homer

unmirrored line piercing
electric where lovers

fall through their perforations riven
by indigo orphic

I like to swing out over its edge

dimorphic nymphalid in your inflections
lake draped

in one half hour I can walk off the earth

Jagged tethers of oxygen
Heraclitian surf

you hear slapping rosaries
shaded sunflooded target

in the sand in the swim
au revoir

ride harassing
seas if you want to pleat them

speech gust

ink in me
erotic

phonetic young
afterlife

Cezanne's cubes of light
Camille's lovers

slit indigo
cantilever Turner's gold seep

delicate pink composed
yellow to its limit blue to its wait

carved regardless
to the edge I could see

water divide I could row out
could hammer the all merciful

tumbled prayer
lovers as rivers are in that world

little detail in middle of scroll
unspooling

god on the bank one

day the god
reaches down am I salt

water keen extravagant light pummeling
anything born

Sand tapped by hand
psychedelic adjacent

tantric
scalpel your hand stems

the clamor
immobile from a swarm of words

your hand calmly draws the two
forms blossoming

I pluck you from the rope
among suns the abstract

night I slip into
soft and vago

108 definitions
not one mention of the poppy

Quiet now a dark among all dark
I can see

always a fluctuation
let alone and unarmed

libido
whose action there is less

anamnesis so
its abyss to which I am kin

You find the bowing

silence dying solo
her privacy

if she approaches
must this text

bird with its turns
written on the undersides

further the anonymous
destinies of art the window

has lifted I float
aerated, drinkable

All that is left

called to the games of time
as the stars in summer

grammars I slipped through
imperceptibly in this latitude

an instant then dark
anonymous dreaming its structure

swiftly from my eyes
I make out where we lived

remember wave and wait
virgin

You view the sea
air as Lascaux unspoilt

relay to mended eyes
extended in the eastern curve

you statue-like
hooves positioned in

a silent wall
fever murmuring

do not hurry
walking or sleeping come

from above delicate
blindness as the whirl

wind suddenly
seeps soon I die soon I enter

another hermetic your body
you seize

the poem carried
where only the mind wings the both

solitudes scrap what
is no longer you

Whose expanse engulfs

the god-like loner
her whitegray whitetone

singularity just
Plato a composition

trippy verse in the shade
the clays breathe

inside me on her back
in her skin steep

eyes only what wings see
wash the frescoes

scale thrown

Sappho lung carved

androgyne
indigo root its incongruous

no-dimensional clamor
to the stem

rupture a blue no longer
far from me the sea

wouldn't it
the patient cache

hoist the god

on the shell clamorous under salt
relieved of its weight

great vocabularies from each
arm climbing the glassy

suppose you partake

Twenty years in the sugar bed
peculiar

grace of a Shaker chair
and Daedalus' vibrances

of air collide
stony escarpment glisten

bittersweet your lips after countless hours
serve me the future

atlas you line with hands
brief while

I have the god and can take that bite
into the clay

your breath has loved
pure pigment stars I did

photograph the churchyard
stark in my arms from the start

AVIARY

The ruin is eight miles by trail

whose pleated flight and song

of unimagined existence and my self

innocent of such twistings

bird lung kite touch

me in bone sunbath

on tender shoots blisses incubate

I am gentle I am alone

crossed by sea water

light and action poured from

wings that are

cambered touching her

self-twisting flight

Half-wild keep

me in god coherent form

spare no

arbor of expression

In the background of the small

picture cry of light

in river grass swamp grass

hummingbird you

come upon the mute

trail toward home

of pleasure faintest

Amber on hills the day across

the cooling spasm pushing

bicycle near shore of unsayable

leaf spray are the stars

streaming to exhaust one another one

of the women is out of breath

or laughs

The lamp stands on the little table

and the little table is spread the bed

in a near total darkenss in which I first

know you undo the garden exceeding

happiness after each flush

all around us ships

called bluets and innocents

Nothing more is desired

nothing is wanting here

is this small salt

sunspun white deeply bent

and a ribbon in her hair please

translucent white through which

sunlit mall of your back

What if there were no sea

to take up the table of our hearts

breath which is everywhere curved

hand from infinity broken

HELEN GROVES

Went walking and walking

far off to get water

two people with your birds

mirrors for multiplying light

we serve

Peaceful limbs

had been little breathless

branches of two humans

the gods are open mouthed

I saw her foot

then a church burning down

with its figure of water then star starkness

she is all I was dead but I was born again

head to guts in her blanket

Islandlike in the morning

she bathes in wet beaver creek

waiting for the sun to warm

limestone boulders dark lip

Where I presently stand my heart can see

peacock overnight then morning quail

how long the sex on your fingers

even when the hand stopped breathing

By long kiss the icon is

worn a lighter color

than the rest of the face

bathing the living

In the turning of the sun she is the scalding path

faith tender muscle

It's not the herbs on my lips

we have freedom to be

infinite or not at all

infinite or not yet

I don't know virgin

when I was made I was made

I am optimistic I am scared a little

what really matters is realism now incurable

too the environment produced from our feelings

my friend it is possible

to drink the ecstatic one's ecstasy

over the source of energy I drink it

I set my sailors east toward our island

took remains of a watermelon lunch

I ask her to help me out of my body

at end of hunger so few needs

wind flies ahead

After barns and wild growing

along fern bank

pairs of young sparrow are hollow I sit in

plus your small loud stream whose birds

I may obtain forty days

mirror pure

I come single

alone

under my clothes

And the cure

ready

ready for you

do I mean

on your body

the wafer

Pod of whales in the heat

beautiful torsos nearby

I have watered you

Our day begins in preparation of the silence

the silence is us

daily I want nothing nothing but this dispatch

Exits everywhere entrance touched your face

after multiple helpings my heart works perfectly

my head far overhead not far from the fantastic

deep sacred racing about

in the acre of fire makes vessel

Where I unbind my hair light's first blue witness

Desert silence

who must constantly beat

her wings

You'll like the worshippers

the sky with its seacoasts of Greece

what kind leaves home for home

send me

VOWEL IMPRINT

Transitive body this fresco amen I mouth

Directly behind door are sandalwood hibiscus

birdhouses in the rain on open land

I make a new one using scrap

for us

Will these floors burst in oxygen

my life spent swimming

inside the cleanest house cleanest bed

sleep of envy probing the ranges of light

nutrients from side to side

infinity acquisitions

How can my body not be sorrow shoulders light

against lips held for hours

and hours the flute

cranes in their nests

You feel the bruising midflight as one born

to dazzle god with your own heat

beside me on the bed your foot

taken into my mouth

I tongue the injured core of its birthright

and the hot burning off of self which exhausts it

Across her veining

luminous between the primaries

where slender swim of harrier and swallow heats air see

how I tie you with water brought from the sky of the unbeaten

burn water for bathing lightly the blind

skin of the pupa leaving it naked but not wanting

like the birds of the holy uncovering young

to the salt of the undersides

Sometimes I don't put away the tools

ripened in shade by the ruined house

with its own whiteness walking upland

neighbors stood and watched it

watched it some more

leafless trees bore shadow

darker in the pasture

the tops of our bodies were hard

ball of blood sent rolling and not shy

I like to be your digging stick

marital female mass

Arresting melancholy seeking to touch

slavery with medication

art calms

Like flocks of solitudes surrender

a bird beautiful and uncovered

I bite small seas into your heart

populate with birds a sky

immaculate with shriek of wing

for its updraft I have married

FLOWER PARRY

Clear blue temple I'm taken in

clear blue temple I'm taken in

god would talk if I did

god would talk if I did

got a mouth wants to know

I was seeing someone burst open

I was seeing someone burst open

the door she was being

the door she was being fucked

hurt as a virtue

hurt as a virtue makes me

vertigo piss-scared

seeing someone burst open

god would talk if I did

Sophia I said I have amassed

the mysteries

let go your hammering

I can aim in any direction and miss

and miss every time

with effort

I can miss with effort

back of my hand

back of my head

no matter how painful

dancing in your mirror

because it is my mirror

if it came from my heart

Walked toward the garden

I had work to show it

then I understood the garden was destroying it

and that I should rest and not water the

shoots in the dark but wait until dark to

uncover them

Rich red euphoriant pumped by heat

at high magnification

in the lightest scan

sweat kicking dense now

the indescribable screams of the ego cleansing

How could I hide from talking tree

I threw that stone at the silent world

and had the sensation

of having killed

nothing feels better

to be certain about

this within

You who are being titillated go

thrive on the tiled plaza to the sea

don't breathe our air into the dark

anti-lips eyes tongue

how come you play for maggots

when juice of air itself gives law

touch my throat I will shatter

god with restraints I'm not

I hope I go dizzy on sight

I broke no law

snip at my soul it's a relief

I know I frighten nurses

headstrong human bundle nodding

and smiling pointing to her eye

showing a picture of singing skull

less than a moment ago the fear of dying no

of killing a homosexual

Passed on by kicks its name is bad

bad doors and windows do its work

court after who courts after

I am more stupid where it strives

first it then me the power of the cage

tamper spoil and lose its asp

split breastbone that was my life

on panic

Pour down avalanche of palms

someone's pulses aim to do as soon as possible

lightening the feet dressing the lips

tenderfoot seedbed in the spirit given rights

over vast agreement

praising floor carried over fields

Practitioner without practice asylumed by her side

at first death and afterlife or even contact craving

frightened me but in commonlight at the lamphole

angel eyebright charge of dreams

shaking the vulgar tablecloth each of us

her splendid gaze mantle burning

I don't know why I serve or want to dance wake up be born

watching the window settle on compassion

I made a wing which we are flying

mountain covered with saints

nice of them to leave the baskets

no moral life is without

individual years creating embrace

how easily it could has changed one bit

I do myself o solitude

at the birthing of sea level

my undesired you ask undestroyed

YOUR SACRED IDIOT WITH ME

Resting is possible

whose shock fills my mind

past once then the real

After the roots have spoken

your night cries

Look after me true

true wherever

A soul I did insist upon

I live superimposed

I have procreated

unless writing

studies the image

and no more

Without a hint of choking

without hesitation

ethical in our nerves

hugging and squeezing

a brain that keeps

ejaculating molecules

in the visible

time poets shine

Came to earth just earth and nothing else

then spirit was born clear easy guest

equal during exposure second

Wonderful mineral like lemon being eaten

in my gums filled with saliva

your translated trance I am performing it

asylum through my clearest my solid birthright singing

full time mercy break god

JOINERY

Long my heart has been

home you feel the most

my arms will tell

Unconscious pocket like new grass

in time of war

you dig one hole I fit rock

I didn't cover myself

I looked instead right back

Art is climax over conduct

zen of no color by sunrise I do

Here at the threshold we took off our cloths

and though I don't remember everything I remember the place

I first saw death seeking a wound and since then one other

sensually nothing I can by now recognize an injection of sleep

spinning clobbered with substance

willing to be sung

I stand in the dark

like photography beaming

the fruit measures itself

asking with my hands

yet more explicit

word with god

Small garden greatest garden I write out

your passions though what I noticed was a jolt

once again this idea I enjoy forgiving

High sky I fell and I forgot cover our tent

you know you shade me

shovelful of pebbles getting lighter at the bedside

losing my hospital vocabulary because just

my everyday fear you hold by the stem

Our maker's void I silence boulder why do you quake

light over here moves her hand

road kill like myself

massive daylight in the grave mass grave

Cure for water is water

one very blue throughout the trees

divine indulgence yesterday

the cross dove from the wall

naked cross get into lifeboat

reincarnation or not

Antennae in the shale with big

microphones jacked in our jewels

remote from sensing eye in sky

human kindness there's a light

drifted far out I can help it

echolocate

I'm done reading your book and admiring you

grape-sized obedience

scaffold with force like sandblast

inside and out minderror mirror

I was silly finding good

your idea

The scary thing gets nervous when I lift it

I spent enough on that

kid harness well oiled

on the lawn spread gravel

for the skinless with salt

Fondest maker I wake up in the dark

hoarding speech behind unknown tongue

Was earlier girlhood a child I might disown

others throw stones to exhaust their restlessness

searchless graveyard sown by kin

whose sleeping and doing

organs color and form the first garden

earth has two worlds

wake and start

On faith from some artist's image

a sheet of paper saying you are possible

I thank the artist for that

island continent its small aborigines

values I stand on I invent

and in the very middle of that gap

the givers

DIGESTIBLES OF SUN

Don't ever cut me from your hands

take all your drink from me

dry lips from the turning kiss my own

fleece from the flock as one true compass

to bear the overpowering morsel

never goes off

Give me your hand candidate for the light

the light won't wake you

nor the fragrant wetting just begun

to join the litany of the visible

we go in and out of the lung

My thinking is play

my writing is play

child don't change species when it know

the physical properties of rainbow

Language you surge

language you try me

I set a place for you

who would have guessed there were so many

similars you with your light

plotted across my window

we are walking toward it arm around

shoulder what else

Because I am preparing

because it is not possible

you bruised me making the indelible erosion

in the blood part seas part cries

as a body sixty-two days of no rain

found its way to life

from the waist down one nightwinter

slips a hand into the clay and digger

Burnt both hands waiting for you

still unwashed

sheet scent let it be my hands

leading you

You've illustrated medicine

what amulet will I keep

I see the hammering of my heart

the sea galloping and galloping

I fail to camouflage myself

in the movable letters of the book

I keep on working the sea to its own headfirst shape

right up to my window

I wouldn't go to my knees

broken bones on my tongue

talk I listen

May you always sing in the way of paint

of which many are vowels as well as colors

rest and be truth in sound and play

be its phonographer

for its own sake for poetry

find again what you have known with

a deer's small pelvis fostering range

as field is cream of a long river

Mistaker repeat the mistake

ignore my close attention be

blind to the silence of eyes

I heeded your great activity

every sinew every point all

the firings little gray

panels of light I heeded you

Who's watching my heart

earth expected many

of the one in my temple

with the steel short hammer and the flare

I dare take you up again

three quarters of every day in the irrepressible acre

Stunned a crimson flower sudden

but not surprising the sunny addiction

the barely possible thirst

Sprig then when stronger leaf

I lie all night with her

I live where she is many

committing cleanness

the chosen chemical suffusing the harm

to the end of helping city

I'm on the side of I spread myself around

I look forward to it

I get on my knees

As in the tender fluted draft of her boneless

inland deep and shoal

slow and seafloor

direct and slanting between elegy and

rush the running of young sap

spit sharpened so her tongue

finds the newly torn

INSOMNIAC OF A ZEN GARDEN FRUIT

Mortal in things I want to pray with you

sleep that rests face to face

so few sympathetics

untroubled by modesty or shame feel your pearled

halo from dreaming sleep that rests

Molecules learned healing people came to drink

Birth becomes familiar

I spit on the rocking wings

Never metaphoric

same tiny hole someone has seen

and has remained

to admit it

I was born easily at home

broken habit of mother

I weep

that is all

PHOTOVOLTAIC

Lord let me all I can wild cherry

I'm dazed all my ways of arriving bear tracks

failure of being torn to pieces is me

mumbling anxiety and I love my heart

I do each day lightly suffering desire

for kindness vividly today

idiot red unselfish green blue threadbare of cloud

outside the labyrinth imagining my life

Write poems

starve off death

Isn't the earth warm

the dew stars and the whole

yours for more work perhaps

inside we change work changes

Lord the voice was large

lord the voice is large

begging even

I had no other dream

I reported back

for this large meaning

bent this way that vernacular with me

Eden after melancholy

palms suddenly heralds

Insistent love I won't outlive the words I lamb in your mouth

anachrist of the bewildered touch of extreme hands

Empty of shit the race is on

empty of eyes made of wood with indifference

don't you straighten it

don't pretend your mouth is not on fire

that stupidity bursts the needle

absolutely on the solid floor

race for the oar light sleeps to dream

travel through shining the ration before you

for every hurt be my large palm

Poetry

SAPPHO'S GYMNASIUM

Outside memory worship never dies

That wish to embrace the great poplar

I woke and my bed was gleaming

Trees fill my heart

Torn mist doves I will love

Light struts cannot be broken

Make praise populations will last

"I have a young girl good as blossoming gold

her ephemeral face I have formed of a key

dearer than skylark homelands"

A full twelve hours like a toiler like Lorca

archaic to bone we parse lark grove

Dutyfree dove seapitched Eleni

nectar your carafe seafounder

Preumbilical eros preclassical brain

Limblooser sweetbitter's scale holds the hem

kitesilk the mind at your ankles

Tides and grape-heaver grammar owl

more soft than agapanthi erotopythons

Her face could still last tone of swaying habit

as if by accident the sea

exactly

Spasm my brakes

downhill oaks

eros wind

Beacon praise

hourless night

poet-taken

Pansappho unscalp unfleece unscalpel our kin

Lesmonia, Lemonanthis, Lesaromas, Lesvaia

Bird is drunk inside me

remembering the smell

at your door

You are the guest

heart traces

Out loud you fill

that doesn't exist

Justice missed hyperventilates poet

Buddha vowel in Mohammet child dared cross

far from mother olive groves father almonds

lyric sap of maple far from Lesvos

The soul has a knee

Just risen just rinses

Laurel to air I speak your lips

Lantern in the abyss

I am what astonishment can bear

tongue I owe you

Pupil only to you

fleece of dew

Small iconostasis clay girls

recombine danger and Homer

In the dark before the candle

where the archetypes take our unconscious to build

the work is forever

Wanderer gathers dusk in mountains

to its end the wind the stream

only riverbank hurry me

Only poetry

SAPPHIC I AM/ BESIDE MYSELF/ A RAPTURE
Kazim Ali

No matter how much religion is organized, the very wild
act of an individual human soul married to a physical body,
attempting to whisper its breath into the universal mouth of
endlessness would be impossible to buckle down to one form,
impossible to write into little books with definitive versions.

This is why, perhaps, whole councils of bishops struggled
to create biblical canon, or Caliph Umar ordered all variant
transcripts of the Quran (until that point an oral text) collected
and burned in order to create an official written version, or
why rabbis argued across space and time in the Talmud,
prefiguring by *thousands of years,* as pointed out by Jonathan
Rosen, the modern phenomenon of the internet.

Instead utterance of the spirit must escape free like the screams
of Antigone or Electra in the ancient Greek plays. Between the
human and divine there is a place where language breaks, not
where it "fails," only where it cannot be tracked "logically,"
i.e. by "word" alone. Such a place too might be called god.

Olga Broumas and T Begley created *Sappho's Gymnasium* in
a collaborative act. They describe their process thus: "But
who speaks? A voice of pluracination, heard partially, as
always, gracing one of us with particulars, the other with the
hallucinated breath of verbally unintelligible but musically
incontrovertible diction. That was one time, which recurs.
Another is certitude of the field it requires us to serve —
eros: gracious, philoxenous, augmenting, lubricant,
remorseless faith."

Every space between two bodies, I once thought, was a place
of danger. But if there is a danger, it is the danger of losing

one's own self, risking transforming into the other. We want to hold ourselves close. But in between the bodies of the two women, or — as Olga explained to me — words originating in the mouth of one (Begley) and passing through the breath and mouth of the other into syntax and structure (Broumas), a third voice, not "disembodied" but actually "re-embodied," issues forth. A collaborative voice, a collective one, not unlike the Greek Choros, but unlike the Choros, which is a public an external voice one that proceeds from a place of intimacy, from logos and eros and ecstasy.

There are three versions of *Sappho's Gymnasium,* written variants on what is essentially an oral text, an unseen *performance.* None of the three may be considered "definitive," only some came before and others after. The first was published in 1994 and the second was included in *Rave,* released in 2000. There are countless large and small differences — about fifty that I myself counted — between the editions; The third version, the one you hold now, diverges similarly but even more radically in that it is a re-shaping of the original version and includes new material.

Think of these three as birds wheeling — first in formation and then flying apart. Or think of them the same way we think of texts of Sappho herself — the written is only a trace record of what was once sung, the musical and embodied as the *real* but also the immediately dissipated, the written is only an archive or a score from which ought to be mined future performances in breath and time.

The original text opened with a quote from Sappho, the spirit-muse who rules the roost here, for more reasons than one: "Tears unbecome the house of poets." The transformation here — a rejection of grief or stasis, an embrace therefore of *ex stasis* or "ecstasy" — poetry, really — is by negation or "unbecoming." Unbecoming means to stay in a newborn state or to travel backward even earlier, to whatever that formless state might be, whereas to be "ecstatic" is to be outside of one's own "self" — however that self be constructed.

What house would a poet live in? The gymnasium where one is "nude, trained, exposed" is a school here of language, of joy and poetry. The body utters and the intellect, the part that wants to organize these prayers into sense, is left behind or at least suspends itself for a moment.

"Any utterance runs the risk of being ideological," Roland Barthes wrote, as invoked later in the "Proem" that opens the book. Here the poets, always plural, want to reject the "thought police" and "recorded grammar" and move out on their own, see what can be discovered while — here two make one — lost in the woods of language.

We came to this new book after long years. I studied at Sappho's Gymnasium myself. I recited this book out loud to myself in the revised New York City of late-autumn 2001, wondering how I could make sentences again. I read Darwish and Broumas and Hillman and wondered what a "city" was any how and what was a "poem?" I saw an advertisement for a poetry workshop to be given in Provincetown. I went.

I came upon Olga like one enters a cave and hears the echo of breathing. I heard her out loud before my eye ever saw a letter she inscribed. Oral and aural and I felt licked, like a baby, like a lover, like a thing being tenderized for consumption. Easy to say on the tongue — tongue is spiritual, sexual, material and in Olga's sounds (her poems are sounds) it is all three, none and one. She retreated into the shadow after reading but later when we talked we found we each had secret Egyptian roots.

I followed those roots and routes out to Cape Cod for a
weekend where Olga taught a workshop about vowels
and breath about how poets lived inside sound. She had us
chant our own names but without consonants. She had us
pronounce them in our mothers' voices. She forbade us to
speak during breaks. What kind of poetry workshop was this?
When at last I tried to read my poem to the group she stopped
me and asked me to sing instead. I sang it. Sang I sound still,
still in days and years that stretch since then, my ear resounds
and swells.

She made a space in me or she uncovered it or she uncovered
my eye to see it. Either way the way I reckon she beckon and
where she Mother and lover beckon, I rebel-son still singing
and reeling do love her and follow. No fallow no fall ere I fall,
err and follow.

> Spare no one
>
> arbor of expression
>
> every day could become
>
> psychotic autistic mute fantasizing
>
> [...]
>
> best friend and half-wild protector named
>
> comfort for the body I can always
>
> pray keep me in god coherent form
>
> of light like memory also distributed
>
> where it is not dimension only[1]

Each phrase can leak into the other — god as best friend and
half-wild protector? Did he (always lowercase in this book)

comfort the body? And what is the prayer: to be kept in coherent form or to be kept "in god" and what is coherent — the body or the form of light; these two perhaps can be said to be the same thing — at any rate, body, god and light all wish to beyond the fact of mere "dimension" or physical shape.

The tender body, the one that is mortal, the one that dies, needs a tender god as well. The human, understanding this walks "out onto the ice finite and helpless in return his soft/ parts ventral know to die." It seems a bitter lesson to learn — that after this glorious awareness, after learning to love one must (we all *must)* learn how to die.

But that fragment is from the part of the book not included here. I sing back to it, just an echo, a seed which flowered forth in new writing —

> this helpless desire your own suffering the
>
> work of grace makes us visible
>
> flocking on small
>
> islands of inland waters the near
>
> shore of unsayable
>
> is your soul[2]

The usual religious practice of seeking "grace" does nothing more than make humans "visible" on their little islands that hover near what cannot be expressed. The drama of the section "Prayerfields," the section which opened the book in its first version was to seek to understand not where one body ends and another begins — it was this dilemma that caused Atalanta to lose her wrestling match (and with it her sovereignty) to Meleager — but rather where the human and mortal part ends and the endless spirit matter begins. Is this the border between life and death? Not "life" nor "death" the way we think of it anyhow: solely in terms of the physical body that we can touch and smell and taste and hear and see.

So how does one return then to a work long since uttered? Does it have life still or do the fragments remain, not to be re-voiced? And not only re-voiced but might *new* voice spring forth once again? Orpheos could not look back at Euridike so one knows the song *will* be different. The process of new lyrics sung forth would not be archeology — the unearthing of new Sapphic fragments — but instead an affirmation in sources of the original in what spins new.

And what spins new nearly twenty years later is rapture. I went to ask the poets if they could sing anew. They only said they would try. Some time later, Olga wrote to say that:

> "We have not been able to bring our recent work through to what might have served as a complementary lumens to the original book.
>
> Distance, my inability to travel to train with her, which is always a thorough source of passion & insight for us, my preoccupation with adjusting to new limitations without wholly succumbing to them, & the terminal illness of friends have intervened to curb our fluidity into the common tongue.
>
> While writing & revising have happened, we don't feel it approaches the seamless lyric of Sappho as it stands."

I believed in what she was saying — that the book still thrummed and new work could not be inserted into it. Creation is vital in time. I understood it as well — I too had been silent as a poet for nearly two years and had no idea whether new poems would come again or not. At the end of

the two years I had written only two new poems. I went again
to Cape Cod to stay with Olga for a few days. My own voice
as a poet had evaporated — it was this loss that led me back to
Sappho's Gymnasium to seek new poems. I read the new poems
to Olga. Upon my return home she wrote to me:

The opening of "Legislature"

thickens my mouth other than how flows
forth from it

& also my memory your voice separating aged
barn boards flooring the bedroom above us ~~

Thank you for the gift your round
mind reasoning comely as the round

Etruscan eyes your tribes port across sands
of centuries & decades to my stationed

door

Collaboration happens between poets but is an active force
in poetry at all times. And in the meantime, as Olga and T
prepared the manuscript I wrote my need to her. When I told
her I wasn't sure I was a poet anymore she responded with a
photograph of herself in her shower, rivulets of water flowing
down her like amniotic rain. When I wrote to her that reading
poem out loud to her had sent me back into working with
words, she sent a photograph of herself in coveralls holding a
power-drill.

Then came a message from Olga — they had started writing again on Cloud and speakerphone, pages were being written and spoken. And the poetry they created in the electronic air became another new sequence called "Optica." Even the poems from "Prayerfields" were being harvested now — the birds and sky flew forth into a new poem called "Aviary."

A life reshaped: the book uttered between younger women in physical proximity: voices can be whispered into the ear or across the skin. The previous book began across the body but the new book, the one spoken into the air across miles — one lover in the desert of the southwest, the other in a house on the cape — is a book that begins in vision and in distance:

> The voiceless farther out scarred with ravines
>
> outplaying doxa
> on broken tablets the groves
> prevent the eye from stopping

These poems may rove constantly in their perception but that does not mean their vision is superficial or too peripatetic to offer insight; rather, there is an instant intimacy, a recognition of the other-as-self

> you are shadow
> hello shadow

The mouth is a staging point here for perception; the consonants and open spaces of the vowels ask to be pronounced — "fall through their perforations/ riven by indigo orphic." The eye as it perceives and the ear as it fills with the "phonetic young/ afterlife" of these poems are joined by touch, smell and taste to create a full sensory and gymnastic experience. While the previous incarnation of 1993 opened with poems that named god as a "jailer" whom the poets asked to "burn the river down," here the abjection of humanity as it relates to the divine is part of the gift:

God on the bank one

Day the god
Reaches down I am salt

Water keen extravagant light pummeling
Anything born

The earlier opening sequence depicted a tension between the desire of human to find a divine in which to rest and the desire of a parent or a sibling or a lover to negotiate the terrain of togetherness or separation with the loved one. One poem from the earlier version speaking of childbirth says of mothers "borderlines they need," and that in "movement of her own/ body she wishes to be small/again" yet in the new poems, conversely, it is the poets who are being *born:*

Quiet now a dark among all dark
I can see
[...]

its abyss to which I am kin

[...]

I make out where we lived
remember wave and wait
virgin

The poems of "Optica" fly high in the air and low over the water, like wheeling birds. They fill with light and space of newborn perception. Their gods are Eros, Sappho, Dedalus, Aphrodite, gods of deep fervor, messy gods, all gods who spill or have been spilled.

They lead on their wings to what feels like a shocking evaporation, condensation and distilling of the poems from "Prayerfields": the lines that streamed through space and condensed again built into new material — a poem of birds and blue and sky that form "Aviary."

The nine short lyrics that make up "Aviary" draw images, phrase fragments and sometimes full lines from "Prayerfields," but their presence here is more of an evocation of the previous poem than a restaging of it. Countless poets and translators since Sappho have tried spinning her fragments out into full poems and Broumas and Begley almost seem to be following the same practice here. The first lyric even evokes a ruin out in the wilderness accessible only by trail.

The trail here is the breath of the poets, their own memory of the lines they once recited. And recitation here is not solely by mouth but by full breath. Lungs made an appearance in the previous sequence and they appear here too:

> Bird lung whose action
> never metaphoric
>
> […]
>
> on tender shoots blisses incubate

Not only do the poets deny the metaphor, they ask the reader/ listener to be in the space where grammar, image, poem itself all go wild. And "wild" here isn't a metaphor either — the birds themselves see to that.

While in the previous incarnation of "Prayerfields," the poets stayed down in the earth and explored the concepts of borders and boundaries, in "Aviary," birds help them fly free. Sometimes the fragments brought forward from the previous book are radically repurposed. The first lyric I quoted before appears in "Aviary" like this:

> Half-wild keep
>
> Me in god coherent form
>
> Spare no arbor of expression

Part of the power of all the poems in the book is how grammar slips across the line, forcing multiple meanings to bloom the way bulbs can be forced in early spring. In the first version of this utterance one might imagine being kept "in god" like a "coherent form of light" or like "memory," but in the second version the prayer is to be kept in "god coherent form." And rather than the invocation to the arbor to "spare no one," the notion now is that the "arbor of expression" — a worldly coherence, a poetic coherence — is to be avoided in order to attain understanding. There is no best friend or protector left in the new poetry.

We come to language through existence then, or said more directly, through actual breathing. It's the selfsoul here that takes you through; rather than the notion that and one has to be handled, anointed, or baptized — validated by some external office — we move out, like birds into the wild world, into the "sunspun" and "transclucent white."

From the broad open space of the boundless sky to a more concentrated arboreal venue, the opening section of "Helen Groves" sets the stage for the drama to come:

> what if there were no sea
>
> to take up the table of our hearts
>
> breath which is everywhere curved
>
> hand from infinity broken

The poets question what the individual will do without the infinity outside and beyond. Now turned inward how could one *not* feel lonely? One does float after all in the saline sea. The "floating" is not merely superficial (one floats by taking enough air into the lungs to remain buoyant — one only sinks, and thus drowns, by taking water into the lungs) but deeper even that that: the result of millions of years of evolution since our emergence from the ocean, the salt content of blood and seawater remains precisely identical. The "heart" then of the sea and the body is the same, a table on which one floats.

What if our anxiety — the anxiety of death, of what will happen to us "after" — is the same as the anxiety of the soul *before* birth: will we be received? What happens on the other side of this existence? Like the question of who we are in a dream this one remains unanswerable. Breath turns in the lungs the way space bends in the universe. A human body is fashioned out of another human body and *somehow* in the womb cells transition from tissue into incarnate being. No one can say when and no one can say really how. Human bodies — flesh — "broken" perhaps from the beginningless store of universal energy that is still to this day being categorized and understood — seen for what it really is: none of it has either appeared nor disappeared, it seems, since the very so-called beginning of time. It has always Been.

So the bodies that broke off, the humans, have a role to play:

> Went walking and walking
> far off to get water
> two people with your birds
> mirrors for multiplying light
> we serve
>
> Peaceful limbs
> had been a little breathless
> branches of new humans
> the gods are open mouthed

One delight of the queer line breaks and eschewing of any punctuation is that sometimes clauses lead both backward and forward. Who are the mirrors meant to multiply light, the birds or the humans? And who is being served?

Humans, at any rate, by dint of the vulnerability of our forms, are tasked with the coarser chores of life. The two humans in this case, peaceful, having walked a long way for water, are breathless. It is unclear whether it is during their breathlessness the gods open their mouths or whether *they* themselves are the gods in question. Either way one is left to consider the qualities of being "open mouthed": exertion, intimacy, communication, desire ...

"The idea of a book held me as icons hold others," the poets quote Odysseas Elytis in the "Proem." "I had but to fill it as you fill a row of empty glasses and, immediately, what power, what freedom, what disdain toward bombs and death it gave me." So the book or icon is something to be entered, to be interacted with in some way. Here in "Helen Groves" the poets say, "by long kiss the icon is/worn a lighter color/than the rest of the face/bathing the living."

It is through these physical interactions — birth, a kiss, bathing, caressing, sexual intimacy — that bodies come to know each other. The sun-soaked mythology of Broumas and Begley traffics in Greek idiom, landscape and sensibility but runs counter to the myths of alienation so prevalent in the ancient stories: Psyche who should not look, Eros who would not be seen; Orfeos who should not look, Eurydike who could not be seen; Echo who could not speak, Narkissos who would not hear; Atalanta who did not know where bodies ended, Medusa who could not be looked upon, Cassandra who could not be understood, the Sirens who could not be listened to. And so on.

The speaker here, like Homer's Telemakhos, is unworried by the question of actual "origin." When Athena disguised as Mentor asks Telemachus whether he is Odysseus' son the young man says with the blithe unconcern of youth, "My mother says I am his son; I know not surely. Who has known his own engendering?"[3] The poets here clarify, "I don't know virgin/when I was made I was made," meaning there's no "blank" state or "pure" state, the answer to that old Zen question of "who were you before your parents were born" seems suddenly to be a somewhat stark though simple "No one." Is it too philosophical for the actual and ongoing world? The body with the mind in it, unaware of the infinity or eternity of the spiritual energy inside, is left with few ways to understanding it:

> It's not the herbs on my lips
>
> we have freedom to be
>
> infinite or not at all
>
> infinite or not yet

It's a wonderful little musing, turning away from sensory experiences as a route to spiritual awakening and declaring the right of the human to ignore all this philosophy, to ignore the infinite inside, to be what one chooses to be, though the second choice implies that the awareness is inevitable, one is only left with deciding "infinite" or not yet infinite ...
Though these poets of course dare to actualize. They confess in the very next poem, "I am optimistic I am scared a little" — how lovely to read both emotions in the same line, unmediated by connective language or comma. "My friend it is possible," they go on to say, "to drink the ecstatic one's ecstasy/over the source of energy I drink it."

"I come single," the poets declare in their twin voice, "alone/ under my clothes." "Alone here" has echoes of what we really *are* under our clothes — naked. In this original state, "alone," we arrive prepared for the journey. As one reads an echo of "naked" under "alone," one too hears the sexual *double entendre* in the spare declaration "I come."

The supplicant, washed in the eros of knowledge, ready to light the lamp and stare then at its sleeping body, is given a little motivational speech at the end of the section:

> You'll like the worshippers
>
> the sky with its seacoasts of Greece
>
> what kind leaves home for home
>
> send me

Here the seemingly infinite and intangible sky possesses inside itself the physical seacoasts of the former homeland. But there's no nostalgia in it because the poets dream of leaving "home for home," ask then — who is it they are asking? — to be sent. The body then, though explored as an instrument of liberation, is asking here to be acted upon. How can it be?

Can you believe in both things at once — that infinity is inside but that the self is still separated from it, that you still must beseech that separate thing, pray *to* it?

Prayers in every religious tradition always depend on their being uttered in the "proper" language for complete efficacy, whether — for example — Sanksrit, Arabic, Hindi or Latin. The *intention* of the supplicant is secondary to the breath flowing through and animating the consonants of need.

The word "vowel" from the section "Vowel Imprint" opens with "vow" of course, and opens its mouth to modulate and end on the liquid "l" (a yogic chanter is reminded of pronouncing "Aummmmmm." And the word "imprint" itself "im" "prints" when the close-lipped breath of its first "m" (said by linguists to be a human body's first consonantal pronunciation — in infancy, the mouth surrounding a nipple) meets the "p" (our second sound, the sound the mouth makes upon releasing said nipple).

The imprint of a vowel must be that depression made — on earth, sand or skin — by the breath of another. One also remembers the Islamic version of the story of the Virgin Mary, giving birth under a date palm, alone and ostracized. To give her sustenance the date palm drops fruit into her lap; taking one she expels a breath in pain and the humble date is thus forever imprinted with her breath and made the holiest of fruits.

"Vowel Imprint" contains mostly short utterances or expulsions, some of them only a single line long, as if in effort to pack greater impact into as brief a possible vessel of poetry. Indeed the first line of "Vowel Imprint" is one that has captivated me for years, one which has written itself in breath and in other kinds of ink all along the measures of my skin:

Transitive body this fresco amen I mouth

The vowels of this opening line begin hemmed in by multiple hard consonants of the first word "transitive." They open wider in the word "body," but it isn't until "fresco" with its multiple liquid consonants "f," "r" and "s" that they really open free. The hard "c" of "fresco" causes a little expulsion of the vowel sound. It is notable that the turn from hemming consonants to releasing consonants happens on the neutral word "this." "This" holds a lot of power here — referring to the "fresco," which is of course also the body. The wide open vowels of "amen," "I" and "mouth" open the poem out as breath, though the final word "mouth" of course imitates the body — a vessel container of the boundless open inside — the "ou" in "mouth" is the same as the "Au" in "Aum."

The body is both transitive here, a passage, a bridge of flesh for breath between states of before and after, but also a fresco, made of pieces from all eras of time and all places throughout the universe. If the body is a fresco could it be the eternal matter that is painted onto the flesh of the body? But in a fresco that paint itself has bonded, become part of the wall; they are no longer separable

The appearance of the speaking "I" (relatively late in such a brief poem) is the bridge between internal acknowledgment of infinity — "amen" — and the act of the individual actualizing herself into the external world, the exhalation of breath in "I mouth."

Of course what makes the line *truly* interesting is that it moves beyond standard syntax of prose declaration and into the queer strange language of ecstasy reminiscent of the odd choral ejaculations in ancient Greek drama. It's never fully clear what the subject, main verb, and object of this line are.

Is the fresco being mouthed or the body or is the mouth an open space at the end of the line, mere descriptor for the I?

In the short poems of "Vowel Imprint" there is always a challenge or danger in lingering in the half-real zone between the actual physical world and spiritual awareness. At one point the poets worry, "Will these floors burst in oxygen/my life spent swimming." Later they warn, "You feel the bruising mid-flight as one born/to dazzle god with your heat." The encounters between the individual human and her spiritual sound are fraught with the essential difference between asceticism and human needs, the "hot burning off of self which exhausts it."

How is one, as a faulty human, a hungry one, supposed to continue in the face of such dangers? In the earlier version of "Vowel Imprint," the poets mused:[4]

> Honey of clarity and strength laboring light
>
> the yes of song and its relentless ear
>
> the actual words

The desire toward song, toward affirmation came accompanied by its "relentless ear." The "actual words" at the end may be song or they may be ordinary human utterance. Or it may be — best of all — that ordinary human utterance *is* song if only we could learn to hear it as such.

Thus reassured in the original versions of this section, the poets realized:[5]

> I am not alone
>
> facing the sun
>
> lover of all

But these reassurances are not included in the new prayer; it concludes in air, with the speakers alone, again, committed not to the distant and concrete solar icon but rather to the abstraction of the bird-sounds and the wind into which they launch themselves.

Out of all the fragments and lines and scraps of Sappho there is a single poem to bear witness that Sappho was not mere ancient postmodern poetess marrying broken phrase with profound insight like Myung Mi Kim or Susan Howe. Her single poem shows a musical poet working wonderfully within the musical and metrical conventions of the time, a poet like Dickinson perhaps. So among the shreds and shards of *Sappho's Gymnasium,* around half-way through the book significantly, we come upon the first page of "Flower Parry," a poem written in a more standard performance mode but with all the metaphysical worries and flurries of the poems that came before and that follow.

This opening poem uses repeated lines almost like blues musicians repeat lyrics. It's an apt comparison since throughout *Sappho's Gymnasium* the poets riff on themes, words and phrases:

> Clear blue temple I'm taken in
>
> clear blue temple I'm taken in
>
> god would talk if I did
>
> god would talk if I did
>
>
> got a mouth wants to know

I was seeing someone burst open

I was seeing someone burst open

the door she was being

the door she was being fucked

hurt as a virtue

hurt as a virtue makes me

vertigo piss-scared

seeing someone burst open

god would talk if I did

Is it true then that god demands the submission of the individual ego, so equating spiritual enlightenment with a violence? In which case the idea of being thus "hurt" — that is to say "enlightened" — is not necessarily appealing to the individual person. *Why* should we give up our own individual perceptions, our own distinctive uniqueness? If even under the worst of circumstances we are afraid of change then small wonder we are of "realizing" infinity or immortality.

The line that rings in my ear is, of course, "got a mouth wants to know." Who is it that has a mouth? The human "I"? And what is it I want to know? The poem gives no chance to find out. Is it true that god will only talk if we see someone "burst open"? The thought gives scant comfort. Barring actual god-talk or prophecy the poets are left only with their own powers of ecstasy and utterance. As they said in an essay on the collaboration, "I need a wafer, equal in body and propulsion,

that develops an entirely immaculate congregation of the
tongue so that we might address you in words your love
shapes."[6]

"Flower Parry" goes on to challenge the easy notions of
obtaining wisdom by exploring some of the real dangers
and difficulties that lie in wait for the individual human, the
one who has a body and mind vulnerable to attack. "Let go
your hammering," one poem begins, saying "I can miss with
effort . . . no matter how painful . . . if it came from my heart."
In one place the effort of spiritual struggle is not conscious. In
talking about a failing garden the speaker observes:

> I should rest and not water the
>
> shoots but wait until dark to
>
> uncover them (96)

"God with restraints I'm not," the poets say, as if to re-
emphasize that one is caught in a swing between an
understanding of "God" in strictly human terms and a refusal
to categorize (or capitalize, or capitalize upon) god at all.
There seems sometimes in the swinging to be no in-between
space. In the closing poem the moment of creation and
destruction is explored:

> I don't know why I serve or want to dance wake up be born
>
> . . .
>
> I do myself o solitude
>
> at the birthing of sea level
>
> my undesired you ask undestroyed

It's the unmentionable things there, the reversed things that
exist in the present moment always, actually "unasked" for. In
a quest to reach spiritual enlightenment the individual human

suffers precisely because the body has its sensory limitations, is trapped in a sensory existence. The lustful supplicant is rife with unquenchable desires so how is it possible to move forward at all? The image of the Fool, first card of the tarot's major arcana, seems suddenly to be the position of knowledge, the simple saint, the sacred idiot, the only one able to achieve wisdom.

The lyrics of "Your Sacred Idiot With Me" splinter into brief and compressed two- and three-line epigrams, almost as if devolving into child speech or baby talk:

> After the roots have spoken
>
> your night cries

> Look after me true
>
> true wherever

In these brief moments we are able to grasp or explore insights without some of the verbal and rhythmic fireworks that characterized early sections of the book. The syntax stripped down here, the line breaks less unconventional; yet the extreme compression itself offers a kind of shivering sometimes:

> A soul I did insist upon
>
> I live superimposed

One thinks of the earlier "fresco" here. If we are superimposed though, superimposed on *what*? What is the nature of the connection itself between the material world and the spirit world? Because of there is a duality between them then spiritual search in the material world must be limited to realm of "preparation;" there will be no achieving in the mortal frame of a life. It might be the job of poetry like this to expose the cracks or rents in our perception of the world and the actual physical world to show the places and possibilities where there is actual transit between the material and spiritual. In other words, "in the visible/time poets shine."

In a hymn or choral ode the language transforms from the plainspoken of the rest of the section into the more ecstatic musically infused rhythms of the earlier sections of the book:

> your translated trance I am performing it
>
> asylum through my clearest my solid birthright singing
>
> full time mercy break god

In the first line there is a trance that is given by one person, "translated" from somewhere — from the spiritual realm of formless energy in the absence of matter, meaning *words?* — and passed along to the other who is then able to "mouth it" or perform it. Here then is the story of the writing/speaking of this book, two poets, Begley and Broumas, who pass the words and lines across the space between them.

The words in this case become an "asylum" or "birthright" both of which imply transitional states — "asylum" meaning a freedom from past oppression or sanctuary with other like-minded individuals otherwise unable to function within mainstream society, and "birthright" which means a reclaiming in some way of something intrinsic which has gone unrecognized or has been lost.

When the poets sing "full time mercy break god," god breaks free in the poem. "He" has been previously mentioned by name very rarely but here god breaks at the end of a line, a chain of associations which evinces not worry or apprehension but rhythmic and spiritual release into open expression.

Wood can be joined to itself by pegs which means held together but by its own material, fastened but not splintered, not pierced. In "Joinery" body and soul, matter and energy or human and human thus weld together and become "structure."

"Long my heart has been/home," one lover may say to another, "home you feel the most/my arms will tell." The limbs of the body narrate the story of lust and love here, as in the Quranic story of the body which speaks of the deeds of the person on the Day of Judgment. If the body can speak out (to divine force in this case, one presumes) then maybe the body can speak inward to the self and not in after-time but now immediately in this-time:

> Art is climax over conduct
>
> zen of no color by sunrise I do

Perhaps "intention" or motion of the mind into the physical world is what is meant by "art" here, an art which trumps actual conduct. The second line of the couplet uses the language of the vow. Broumas, a Zen Buddhist, has written elsewhere of her work in massage and its counterpoint in meditation practice. She greets this practice of the body without "color," without intention, each and every day. In her essay "Moon," she says, "I have neither hope nor the absence of hope. I have the sweeping."[7]

It seems passive but in the next poem of "Joinery" the poets praise not willingness to sing but the gift of being "willing to be sung." The body itself, the human life becomes expression of something else ineffable, something with agency. Imagine it: that you are not singer but thing *being sung*.

Other metaphors besides joining, music and meditation throughout this section include photography, gardening and sonar location. The actual spiritual symbols aren't all Buddhist though. In one poem the poets consider "reincarnation" with Christian symbols, meant for all supplicants though, not limited here to god (in the form of the Jesus)

> Cure for water is water
>
> one very blue throughout the trees
>
> divine indulgence yesterday
>
> the cross dove from the wall
>
> naked cross get into lifeboat
>
> reincarnation of not

It's the "not" at the end of the poem, the doubt that quickly questions everything that came before that really drives the point home: No matter what is believed or disbelieved, no matter what poetry works to reveal, the fundamental unknowability of spiritual conditions is wall not to be breached. In other words, "My belief and aggression took so long/sowing ground in her prophetic tropic."

"I'm done reading your book and admiring you/grape-sized obedience," the poets say tartly in the very next poem. What point is there indulging in this so-called minderror mirror, they wonder.[4] "There is no way of rainbow for looking is broke/child behind unknown tongue," they say. It is some reassurance to know it is impossible to have any such revelation. After all the looking eye is "broke." Unlike the knowledge that seemed possible at the beginning when the body first broke from infinity, here it seems the eye *can't* see, won't be able to after all. One puts faith then not in the tongue that can speak in the actual world but the other tongue, the unknown tongue.

The path of the artist — and only that one — can lead the human not to revelations that will fill in the blank of received or expected outlines of the actual confusing world with all of its contradictions, countermandings and, yes, countertexts. "On faith from some artist's image/a sheet of paper saying you are possible," reassure the poets, "values I stand on I invent/ and in the very middle of that gap/the givers."

Once more we are left in the space between the seeker and what could be known. Neither can be achieved. Only the material actual physical world can be sensed and perceived by the human incarnate body. What wisdom there can be can only be achieved in quotidian and ordinary things. The body must know its own processes then — birth, love, breath, age and death — to have any hope of deeper connection. Is it possible? That remains to be seen.

"I AM TASTING MYSELF/IN THE MOUTH OF THE SUN," June Jordan says in a poem, dreaming herself born of that (seemingly) eternal source of (seemingly) endless energy.[8] What's digested by the sun must then be transformed. Anxiety about separation (birth?) and desire for connection open this section.

"Give me your hand candidate of light," one seeker says to another, reassuring "the light won't wake you."[5] There is an in-and-out movement like the tide or breath that enables one to harmlessly engage with oneself and the community at large:

> Language you surge
>
> language you try me
>
> I set a place for you
>
> who would have guessed there were so many
>
> similars to you with your light
>
> plotted across my window

we are walking toward it arm around

shoulder what else

Once again the poem fragments and splinters off at the end reminding the reader there is more to go, that the journey is endless process. Besides an ode to language, of course, it is also an ode to touch, ending with the human connection of one's arm resting around the shoulder of the other. Language and the body meet as one here and in many erotic lyrics that thread and rethread their way through the sequences of the book.

Throughout the three incarnations of *Sappho's Gymnasium*, stanzas appear and disappear, shift from sequence to sequence, sometimes transposed, sometimes rewritten, sometimes reimagined. In dramatic demonstration of what is at stake in this shifting architecture, the three versions of "Disgestibles of Sun have three different endings. In its original publication the searcher feels an erotic or ecstatic moment wondering where boundaries of skin truly lie:[55]

Her hours alone allure

mind makes mind need to cure

our work before us shape to be

receiving skin amid unceasing

By the republication in *Rave*, a previous stanza completes the poem, creating a different and perhaps more pointedly conclusive moment:

I dream in the land

I lose all sensation

I last an instant

sazzling altar

> angels and angels
>
> one church

But by the current version, both of these moments have vanished and a new utterance offers violent hope to the once-again prophetically uttering poets:

> As in the tender fluted draft of her boneless inland
>
> [...]
>
> rush the running of young sap
>
> spit sharpened so her tongue
>
> finds the newly torn

To contrast the earlier image "hand from infinity broken" from "Helen Groves" here we find "spit sharpened so her tongue/ finds the newly torn." The difference between "broken" and "torn" is that the "torn" does imply an external force acting upon a previously whole matter, whereas "broken" may be a present condition which has its own agency, i.e. a small part "broken off" of a whole but also in itself whole. While it may be a Christian idea that liberation is dependent on the external factor, whether "grace" or an actual actor, the Son of God or whoever, there might also be something to thought that other humans are required for the liberation of the individual.

If what's "digestible" is something that passes through the Sun, or the energetic power of the universe, the "insomniac" must be someone unable to interface in any meaningful way with the restorative and intangible energies of the universe. Sleep thus denied though, the conscious mind moves into a different and skewed relationship with the reality around one. "The light upon me a kind of body," the insomniac realizes suddenly in her sleep-deprived clarity, in a fragment from the

132

earlier version not included here. Talking about the woods, she thinks, "the twigs snow soft/fetch knots of spring then eager morning."

It's almost as if, because of its inability to engage, the separated body can detect a greater subtlety in the absences of perception. In this case she is attuned to both the physical manifestation of time ("knots") and the *feeling* of time ("eager") in the motion of spring.

Throughout the sections of "Insomniac of a Zen-Garden Fruit," the shortest in the book, the images of childhood, natural landscapes and marriage presented all along in earlier sections recur and recur as if in waves. One is reminded of the genderedness of certain experiences: in a book written by and in the interchange and exchange between two female bodies, climaxes are multiple. But the newer incarnation ends not in "marriage" but rather in a range of different kinds of female-bodied experience.

The penultimate sequence, "Photovoltaic," does indeed "turn" in "light"; it turns from a pure climactic moment of lingual ecstasy to an earnest injunction to "Write poems/starve off death." It continues to alternate between an address to an outside "Lord" and later "you," and an internal observational voice. The "you" shifts and changes throughout the sequence, and unlike — for example — in Louise Glück's *The Wild Iris* (another work which deals with the traffic between human and divine in which the speaker of the poems alternate among flowers, gardener and god), here it is harder to say (or perhaps better to say the question is irrelevant) who the "you" in any given poem is: a human addressee, the "Lord" or divine element or the speaker herself (herselves!).

It's appropriate to have that level of confusion for a poem that in its first line seems to use the phrase "wild cherry" as a *verb:*

Lord let me all I can wild cherry

I'm dazed all my ways of arriving bear tracks

failure of being torn to pieces is me

mumbling anxiety and I love my heart

"Dazed" indeed, the supplicant finds in this poem her path
intersected not only with "bear tracks" (animal beings)
but also "dew stars," and the earth in repeated iterations.
The ecstatic uncoupled language she actually refers to as
"vernacular" — not the heightened and ritualistic language
of prayer with its human hierarchy of entry (priesthood,
scholarship, etc.) and its imagined divine hierarchy of
reception (who is worthy or washed clean enough for prayer,
whose prayers will actually be answered, etc.) — but rather
the plain speech of those "uneducated," the perhaps always
"unwashed!"

The vernacular is confused, stumbles along (note the inverted
subject in line 3), and moves against the linearity of address
expected in a prayer designed for communal worship. No
"mass" here but individual address, moreover not even
between supplicant and "God" but between two human
women who declare:

I do each day lightly suffering desire

for kindness vividly today

idiot red unselfish green blue threadbare of cloud

outside the labyrinth imagining my life

The "idiot" or wise person again makes an appearance here
suffering, though lightly, desire. The scintillation of colors
seems to belie this suffering; though threadbare or not she is
still engaged in the highest form of praise, "imagining." The

labyrinth, place of confusion and even danger, is abandoned here, and threads — *sutras* or sacred texts, threads the devoted tie around their wrists, threads made to weave tapestries or laws, threads that prisoners can use to escape said labyrinths — all flutter away in the stuttering music and assonance of the praising phrases.

Of course what priesthood, scholarship or institutions offer is precisely this: the *organization* of knowledge, and the "inside"/*insight* of achieved wisdom. When we say "received" knowledge we mean someone has collected it, passed it down, given it *to* us. But *who* has given it to us? As I mentioned at the start of my rapture, the books of the bible were voted on and included based on decisions of a council. A caliph ordered the writing down and binding of the oral document that was the Quran, and then of course he ordered it "ordered." All variant versions were collected and burned.

An ecstatic document, a document passed between two people from one mouth to another, would have to be comfortable with its variants, its impermanence.

And as I've already said the two previously published versions of *Sappho's Gymnasium* differ textually in not just superficial ways. Such differences do not seem to be of concern to the text itself — permanence doesn't have much to add to the seeking of a body for sensual or spiritual knowledge: "Insistent love I won't outlive the words I lamb into your mouth."

At any rate, any text that uses both "wild cherry" and "lamb" as verbs is scripture I'll sign up for. And the text of the section of "Photovoltaic," alone out of all the other sections in the book, was unchanged in both of its previous appearances in print; the current version elides one brief stanza.

Whether or not permanence is at stake, it *is* a seeking: "Empty of shit the race is on," the poets urge:

> empty of eyes made of wood with indifference
>
> don't you straighten it
>
> don't pretend your mouth is not on fire
>
> that stupidity bursts the needle

And then they continue:

> race for the oar light sleeps to dream
>
> travel through shining the ration before you
>
> for every hurt be my large palm
>
> Poetry

"Poetry," at the end is the rescuer then, from the hurt, from the mouth on fire, from the indifference, even from the animal panic of bowel expulsion in times of grave danger. And what is the danger here? Death of the body? Loss of knowledge? The poets who traffic in oral ecstasy are channeling Sappho, of course, but doesn't that precisely outline the problem: the woman who sang, tenth of the muses, whose work was strafed to scraps by sand and war and history. The ancient epic of blood and death and the fall of the city were lovingly tendered from hand to hand, but the songs in a woman's voice, the songs of love and the body and Aphrodite, they drift away . . .

So how then are we supposed to continue on our path? Not by learning the chapter and verse but by bringing into our *own* body the process itself for the searching. And for that you need a school of certain sort.

If one can actually learn to "write" or pronounce out the

words oneself, to lamb them into the mouth of another, then perhaps one can "read" *anything* as a sacred text. "Bird is drunk inside me," the poets observe later.

The final and titular section "Sappho's Gymnasium" opens, like any good school, with a series of dicta. But these dicta are meant not to contain but to open wide possibilities for "misbehavior" for its rowdy rabble of students:

> Outside memory worship never dies
>
> . . .
>
> Torn mists the doves I will love
>
> . . .
>
> Light struts cannot be broken
>
> Make praise populations will last

When the poets say "outside memory," they may mean "besides memory," but they may also mean that "memory worship," or a writing in and through the body, is the thing that never dies, the thing that connects the finite body (not really finite at all because made of the infinite undying matter of the universe which neither begins nor ends and only transforms) to the infinite condition of energy (not really infinite all because subject to the conditions of all matter and antimatter — if space bends perhaps time does as well? And if time does then what *about* energy . . . ?).

Thus laced one to another in a spiral that does and undoes itself endlessly we do not necessarily "read" or "recite" but rather "read" or "recite" but rather "remember" and "sing." Here follows then an epigraph the curriculum itself, fittingly, as delineated in the notes of *Sappho's Gymnasium, "intuited" from* a fragment from the Sappho herself:[9]

> I have a young girl good as blossoming gold
>
> her ephemeral face I have formed of a key
>
> dearer than skylark homelands

The love for the girl is a portal into emotion more dear than even a "homeland." Of this metaphor the poets outline what's really at stake: that human love, connection with another, is deeper than nation, than "home," a surer form of worship than any other. This fragment, by Sappho, enters into the stream of the poem, mixes with the words of Begley and Broumas seamlessly.

In this moment even the eros of the breakdown of linguistic structures starts to disappear. "Dutyfree dove seapitched Eleni," the poets sing to Helen, muse of ultimate beauty, "nectar your carafe seafounder."

Sappho and Eleni — Helen's Greek name — weave themselves into the fabric of Broumas and Begley's own words and in this way there seems a generosity of intent in the text. There is in the poems that follow a real commitment to connection, to actual communication, not solely utterance tossed out into the winds of the world. "Tongue I owe you," the poets say, and they mean both that the tongue is a recipient of a debt but also that the tongue itself *is* the debt that must be gifted to another. Spiritual and sexy at once indeed and in deed.

This form of rapt bodily attention has been arrived at by a long and careful exploration of the body and its possibilities. What happens when one rolls back knowledge of the intellect and seeks instead knowledge of the body and its senses:

> Preumbilical eros preclassical brain

Preumbilical eros would be the one body literally inside the other even *before* the stage of separateness. This is eros not of separate bodies meeting each other skin on skin but swimming *inside* one another's sensory awareness. The preclassical brain is one unhindered by discipline or disciplines, that separation of knowledge that seeks also to problematize and alienate the human mind from the body's most significant physical processes: birth, sexual awakening, grief, ecstasy, beautiful age, death.

And what if life in its limbloosening sweetbitter hem of experience is the illuminated part, then death even after death is diffuse, unknowable and unknown? What if "we" (all part of the same source?) transfuse "ourself" *into* flesh from the unknowing state precisely to do what the body can do: learn and know and with each death carry back a little bit more of that understanding?

"Pansappho unscalp unfleece unscalpel unskin of flowers our kin," the poets sing next. This line sings musically even somewhat more when one remembers that in the Greek Sappho's name begins with a *psi* and is spelled further with a *pi* and *phi*, meaning the first syllable ends with a hard "p" sound preceding the "f" of the second syllable; it would properly be pronounced something like "Psapfo."

When the poets wrote in their essay on the collaboration, "My skin is the volunteer cipher of your emotion," they are not speaking to an abstract other but to me actually. To you. Actually.

And so how could I be surprised then when on the next page I found a short letter, written, I felt, actually to me — six years before I met Broumas in New York City, when I still lived in Washington, D.C., was working in social justice organizing and having panic attacks at my constricted and constricting life, before I had started on the path of poetry at all, she pronounced this verse out loud. And then how could I be surprised when six years later I read this book for the first time and missed it?

Not until late 2010, ten years after I read this book for the first time, longing for mentors who kept leaving me by geography or by death, did I suddenly come across the note, cast directly at me — *me* — from across time:

> Justice missed hyperventilates poet
>
> Buddha vowel in Mohammed child dared cross
>
> far from mother olivegroves father almonds
>
> lyric sap of maple far from Lesvos

I am far from my sources, parental, spiritual and otherwise. I dream my way home. My consonants — the religion I was born with, the rules I learned, the body I inhabit — may be that of a "Mohammad Kazim" but my vowels — the breath that moves through them — are from Buddha, Krishna and from innumerable other places. There was a time in my life when I knew that far from my sources in every way — far from "God" and far from poetry — I would have to make everything up myself, in a language quite before unheard.

This is a book both individual and expansive, both immediately local and quite endless, as open as the wide southern Mediterranean. And why say anything at the end of the essay at all except pronounce more words from traveling; it seems the end of the known universe:

> In the dark before the candle
>
> where the archetype takes our unconscious to build
>
> this work is forever

It is the purest pleasure, warm water, the breeze coming off the sea, the bright sun on the water, the cold blue, to once again swim in this book, to see it again come to light, be glistening, be new.

In the margins of the manuscript as it came to me I wrote myself:

> What lost island cartographers still map
>
> What songs the body remembers
>
> It once could sing
>
> River thinspirate
>
> Unbound
>
> Dark sirens on the rocks

1. Olga Broumas & T Begley, *Sappho's Gymnasium*, Copper Canyon Press, 1996, p12-13.
2. *SG*, p20.
3. Homer, *The Odyssey*, translated by Robert Fitzgerald, p8.
4. *SG*, p89.
5. Broumas, *Rave*, Copper Canyon Press, 1999, p90.
6. Broumas, *Rave*, p362.
7. Broumas, *Rave*, p207.
8. June Jordan, *Directed by Desire*, Copper Canyon Press, 2007, p564.
9. Broumas, 172. Alternate translations of this stanza of Sappho can be found on p89 of the Barnstone translation, p269 of the Anne Carson's translation and is numbered 17 of Mary Barnard's.

An earlier and somewhat different version of this essay appeared as "Third Eye Who Sees: On the Source of the Spiritual Search in Sappho's Gymnasium" in *Resident Alien: On Border-crossing and the Undocumented Divine*, by Kazim Ali, University of Michigan Press, 2015.

NOTES

Our day begins in preparation of the silence / the silence is us:
Roland Barthes

Psapphian: Sapphic spelling of Sapphian

CUPRA: Sapphic spelling of Cypria, Aphrodyte

hetaira: female form of "other"; postdoxic: mistress

Lesmonia Lemonanthis Lesaromas Lesvaia:
real & imagined vocatives/addresses to/invocations of Sappho

T Begley is a poet, essayist, translator, and multimedia artist. Olga Broumas is a poet, translator, and professor at Brandeis University. Her books include *Beginning with O*, a Yale Younger poets selection; *Rave: Poems 1975–1998*; *Perpetua*; and two translations of Odysseas Elytis.

Kazim Ali is a poet, essayist, novelist, and translator.

NIGHTBOAT BOOKS

Nightboat Books, a nonprofit organization, seeks to develop audiences for writers whose work resists convention and transcends boundaries. We publish books rich with poignancy, intelligence, and risk. Please visit our website, www.nightboat.org, to learn about our titles and how you can support our future publications.

The following individuals have supported the publication of this book. We thank them for their generosity and commitment to the mission of Nightboat Books:

Elizabeth Motika
Benjamin Taylor

In addition, this book has been made possible, in part, by grants from the National Endowment for the Arts and the New York State Council on the Arts Literature Program.